A WORKBOOK

IN THE

FUNDAMENTALS OF MUSIC

WITH CORRELATED
EAR TRAINING and KEYBOARD EXERCISES

by

H. OWEN REED, Ph. D.

Professor of Music

Michigan State University

FOREWORD

College administrators in the field of music frequently are depressed by the vast number of applicants for admission who possess only a meager knowledge of music fundamentals. Despite considerable skill on a major instrument, the simplest elements of notation often are unknown. Drill, of course, is imperative before a beginning class in Theory can hope to get under way.

Dr. H. Owen Reed has devoted much thought and work to the problem, and this Workbook is the result. It furnishes an effective system of review for students who need it, and a simple method of instruction for those who lack a knowledge of fundamentals.

It is not enough, however, that this drill be given at the College level. A systematic study of the fundamentals of music must be made much earlier if the student is to function as anything more than a technician during his formative years. The private teacher must devote more attention to notation and ear training. The school music teacher should not dignify his instruction with the name of "Music Education" unless his students receive basic training in fundamentals. To do this, a practical Workbook is necessary - - one that has been tested and proved at the Secondary level. Dr. Reed's book meets these requirements.

Someone has said that "Writing maketh an exact man." Nowhere is this more applicable than to Music Theory. The student who says, "I know what it means, but I can't explain it," simply does not know. Here is a way for him to learn.

April, 1947

Roy Underwood
Director, Division of Fine Arts
Michigan State College

PREFACE

This workbook was designed to furnish the music teacher with a systematic means of presenting the fundamentals of music to (1) the private instrumental or vocal student, (2) a class in high school theory, or (3) a first year college theory class in which a concentrated review of fundamentals is necessary.

In preparing this workbook the author has followed the general movement toward the correlation of harmony, keyboard harmony, sight singing, and ear training. It is suggested that the speed of the written work be held to that of the ear training and keyboard drill exercises that accompany the lessons.

There are times when supplementary material will be desirable, particularly in sight singing and melodic dictation. If this workbook is used as a theory text, it is suggested that harmonic dictation and part-writing be started immediately after the aural and written study of the major triad. The inclusion of such material, however, is outside the scope of this book.

If the lessons herein presented are diligently studied, the student should have little or no difficulty in satisfying the entrance requirements in the professional music schools and college music departments in the United States.

Special thanks are due Professor Roy Underwood and the Theory Staff at Michigan State College for their kind and helpful suggestions relative to the material presented in this workbook. Thanks are also due the high school and private music teachers, and the students who have used this book in mimeograph form for their many practical suggestions: Finally, the author wishes to express gratitude to his wife, Esther Reed, for her valuable advice and service while this book was in preparation.

H. Owen Reed

TABLE OF CONTENTS

TABLE OF CONTENTS

INTRODUCTION

The study of the fundamentals of music must have its beginning in a very brief but clear understanding of the most basic principles of acoustics[1].

Sound, which is a sensation resulting from the stimulation of the aural nerves by some vibrating object, is divided into two general classifications: <u>noise</u> and <u>tone</u>. Noise is the result of an irregular vibration, as for example, the falling of a book on the floor. Tone, on the other hand, results from a regular vibration.

Whereas some musical instruments (for example the drum) make effective use of noise, it is tone which contributes primarily to the language of music. Tone has four properties:

1. pitch ------ the highness or lowness of a tone,
2. duration --- the length of a tone,
3. timbre ----- the quality of a tone, and
4. intensity -- the loudness or softness of a tone.

It is upon the first two of these properties that Unit One and Unit Two of this Workbook are based. Whereas <u>timbre</u> and <u>intensity</u> are an equally important phase of instrumental development, it is the study of the properties of <u>pitch</u> and <u>duration</u> that is necessary to the basic understanding of melody, rhythm, and harmony.

---

[1]The science of sound.

UNIT ONE: THE NOTATION OF PITCH

Lesson 1.   The Musical Alphabet; The Staff; Clef Signs; Notes.

Since music is a language, there must be some means of written communication. Appropriate symbols must be used to convey a musical message from the composer to the performer. The first consideration, in the writing and interpretation of music, will therefore be the study of the notation of the first property of tone -- pitch.

The Musical Alphabet.

Of all the many variations of pitch that occur from the lowest to the highest, in the range of audibility, those in musical usage today can best be illustrated by the piano.

The piano contains the mechanism for setting into vibration tones of varying pitch, all of which are named by the use of only the first seven letters of the alphabet:

$$a \quad b \quad c \quad d \quad e \quad f \quad g$$

Since the pitch of a tone is dependent upon the number of times the vibrating medium vibrates per second, it has arbitrarily been the usual practice to tune musical instruments so that the letter "A" is associated with a tone which vibrates 440 times per second, or some multiple or sub-multiple of 2 of this value. For example, a tone which is the result of 2x440, or 880 vibrations per second is also named "A", the relationship between the two "A's" being called the interval of an octave. A tone resulting from $\frac{1}{2}$x440, or 220 v.p.s., is likewise called "A", the relationship again being that of the octave. (The "A" vibrating at 220 v.p.s. is said to be an octave lower than "A = 440".) Each tone of this series of seven basic tones recurs, in both directions at the octave, until the upper and lower extremities of the instrument have been reached.

The determination of the frequencies of the other basic tones within the pitch range of the "A" octave is beyond the scope of this book[1]. It will suffice here to say that these basic tones (a b c d e f g) correspond to the "white" keys on the piano. The "black" keys represent alterations of these basic tones and are named such as: "A flat" (the black key immediately to the left of "A"), and "A sharp" (the black key immediately to the right of "A"). Altogether each octave is divided into twelve equal divisions.

---

[1]See: F. A. Osborn, Physics of the Home, McGraw & Hill Book Co., Inc., New York, 1929, pp. 95-98.

Drill problems for Lesson 1 appear on Page 51

The Staff.

In order to communicate tones by writing, characters called "notes" are placed upon a staff. A staff is composed of five horizontal lines separated by four intervening spaces. The usual numbering of these lines and spaces is shown in Example 1.

Ex.1

In order to accommodate a greater range, two staffs are used and connected as in Example 2. This is called the Grand Staff.

Ex.2

Clef Signs; Notes.

A clef sign is placed upon each staff in order to locate some particular tone as a point of departure. Upon the upper staff is placed a character called the "G Clef" (or "Treble Clef"). Upon the lower staff is placed the "F Clef" (or "Bass Clef"). The location of these clefs (which is as indicated in Example 3) identifies the two tones from which the clef names are derived. The other tones extend out in both directions from these tones (alphabetically) -- the notes being placed alternately on lines and spaces.

Ear Training.

1. Strike any white note on the piano keyboard within the range of your voice. Duplicate by singing that tone. For example: play middle C -- sing middle C.

2. Strike any white note on the piano keyboard outside the range of your voice. Duplicate that note at the octave within the range of your voice. For example: play the octave below middle C -- sing middle C.

Keyboard Drill.

1. Find and play any given white note on the piano keyboard.

Ex. 8   The Piano Keyboard and the Grand Staff.

Lesson 2. Leger Lines; The 8va Sign.

Notes normally written in the bass clef (Ex. 4) may, by use of leger lines (short lines drawn above or below the regular staff to extend its range), be written in the treble clef (Ex. 5).

Similarly, notes normally written in the treble clef (Ex. 6) may be written in the bass clef (Ex. 7).

To avoid the writing of notes too far above the staff (Ex. 8) the sign 8va‾‾‾‾‾‾‾‾‾‾‾ is used. Notes within this bracket should be played an octave higher. (Exs. 8 and 9 sound the same.)

Extremely low notes (Ex. 10) are written in a like manner, except the 8va---------- is placed below the notes (Ex. 11), the notes within the bracket being played an octave lower.

Drill problems for Lesson 2 appear on Page 53

Lesson 3. Accidentals (or Chromatic Signs).

Each of the seven basic tones (a b c d e f g) may be raised or lowered in pitch by placing the appropriate character (accidental) before the note.

A "flat" $(\flat)$ placed before a note indicates the lowering of a tone a half-step[1], while a "sharp" $(\sharp)$ indicates the raising of a tone a half-step. A "double flat" $(\flat\flat)$ lowers a tone a whole-step[2], while a "double sharp" $(\sharp\sharp$ or $x)$ raises a tone a whole-step. A "natural" $(\natural)$ cancels the previous use of a sharp or flat.

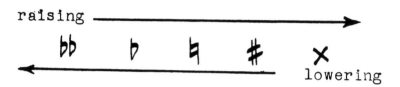

The following chart shows the sharps and flats as they relate to the piano keyboard.

Ex.12

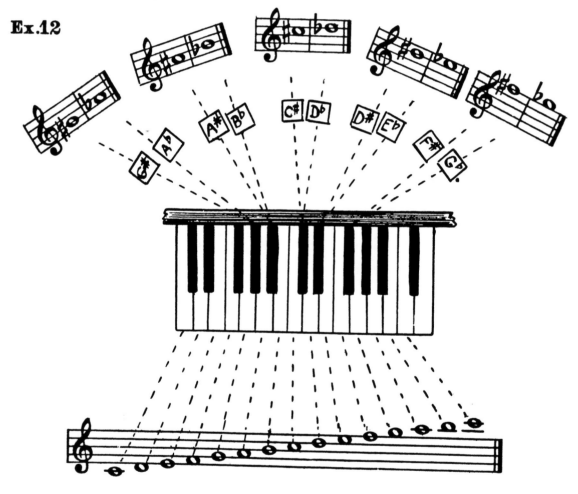

---

[1]A half-step (semi-tone) results from the striking of two adjacent keys on the piano.

[2]A whole-step (whole-tone) is equivalent to two half-steps.

Drill problems for Lesson 3 appear on Page 55

Example 13 illustrates further use of the accidentals.

Ex.13

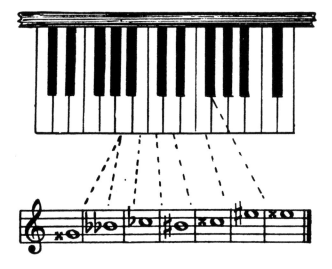

In Ex. 12 the "C#" sounds the same tone as "D♭". Notes which sound the same but are written differently are said to be <u>enharmonic</u> with each other. (For example, CX is en-harmonic with D; EX is enharmonic with F# and G♭ .)

Thus, by means of accidentals, all the tones may be notated. (The reason for the seemingly over complexity of enharmonics will be understood after the study of tonality.)

Ex.14

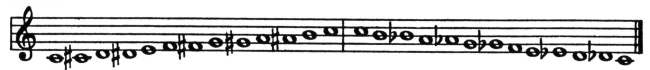

The above ascending and descending series of semi-tones is known as the "C chromatic scale". (Sharps are generally used for ascending chromatic notes and flats for descending.)

<u>Ear Training.</u>

1. Drill on ear training as in Lesson 1. Increase speed.

<u>Keyboard Drill.</u>

1. Play any given note on the piano. For example: Play C# ; B♭ ; A♭♭ ; B# ; C♭ ; F# ; etc.

2. Play a chromatic scale, from any given note, one octave up and return.

3. Name and play the enharmonic equivalent of any given tone. For example: What is the enharmonic equivalent of A# ? Answer: B♭ .   Play B♭ .

UNIT TWO: THE NOTATION OF DURATION

Lesson 4. The Relative Duration of Tones; The Tie; The Dotted Note.

A grammatical statement, in order to be fully understood, must be properly written, with the words accurately spelled and divided to show accent, or else the result might be something in the nature of the "little lambsie divey". Likewise, a musical statement must be correctly written so as to fully convey its meaning.

The second consideration, in the writing and interpretation of music, will be the study of the notation of the second property of tone -- duration. The relative duration of a tone is indicated by the use of various kinds of notes. These notes, their names, and their relative value, shown below.

Whole note   o

Half note   ♩   ½ the value of the whole note.

Quarter note   ♩   ¼ the value of the whole note.

Eighth note   ♪   1/8 the value of the whole note.

Sixteenth note   ♪   1/16 the value of the whole note.

Thirty-second note   ♪   1/32 the value of the whole note.

Occasionally one finds double whole notes (|o|), which receive twice the value of the whole note, and sixty-fourth notes (♪), which receive 1/64 the value of the whole note.

The parts of the note are named as follows:

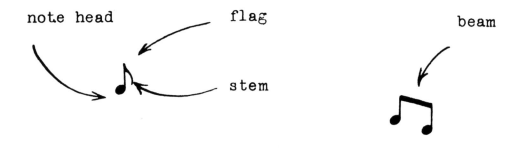

Drill problems for Lesson 4 appear on Page 57

The <u>approximate</u> duration of tones is indicated by a word (or words), usually Italian, referring to speed. For example "Lento" means slowly; or "Moderato" means at a moderate tempo (speed).

A more <u>exact</u> duration of the tones is indicated by a metronome[1] marking. For example, one might find the following:"M.M. ♩= 60" at the beginning of a composition[2]. This means that quarter notes will be played at the rate of 60 per minute. (If the metronome is set at "60" it sounds 60 beats per minute, thus indicating the exact speed of the quarter notes. The eighth notes will therefore occur at the rate of 120 per minute. and the half notes at 30 per minute.)

<u>Divisions and Subdivisions of Undotted Notes.</u>

Ex.15

Unit	Division	Subdivision
𝅝	𝅗𝅥 𝅗𝅥	♩ ♩ ♩ ♩
𝅗𝅥	♩ ♩	♫ ♫
♩	♫	♬ ♬
♪	♬	𝅘𝅥𝅲𝅘𝅥𝅲𝅘𝅥𝅲𝅘𝅥𝅲

It can be observed from the note names (half note, quarter note, etc.) that the mathematical ratio is two to one. Therefore any kind of note can be established as the beat[3], with its regular divisions of two and subdivisions of four.

<u>The Tie.</u>

A <u>tie</u> is a curved line connecting two notes representing the same <u>pitch</u>.

Ex.16

   The second note is not re-struck but played the same, as: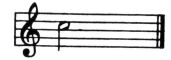

---

[1] A metronome is an instrument which may be adjusted to beat at any desired speed. The scale is calibrated in beats per minute.

[2] "M.M." is the abbreviation for "Maelzel's Metronome", after the name of its inventor.

[3] A <u>beat</u> is "the regularly recurring periodically accented pulse or <u>throb</u> which constitutes the unit of measurement in all measured music"--Webster. The note which received the beat is called the "unit".

The Dotted Note.

A dot placed after a note affects its duration by increasing its value one half.

Ex.17

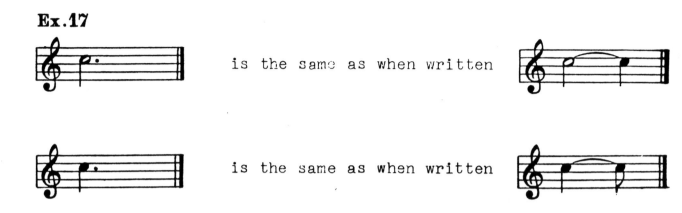

Similarily, a dot placed after a dotted note affects its duration by increasing its value by one half the value of the first dot.

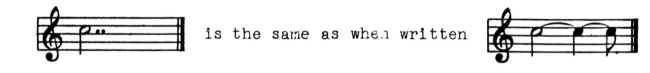

Division and Subdivision of the Dotted Note.

Any kind of dotted note may be established as the beat, with its regular divisions of three and subdivisions of six.

Ex.18

Unit	Division	Subdivision
𝅝.	𝅗𝅥 𝅗𝅥 𝅗𝅥	♩ ♩ ♩ ♩ ♩ ♩
𝅗𝅥.	♩ ♩ ♩	♫ ♫ ♫
♩.	♫	♬
♪.	♬	♬♬

Ear Training.

The student should begin at this time to develop the feeling for the beat, and for the simple division and subdivision of the beat. This can be accomplished in numerous ways, the most direct being tapping exercises. A prerequisite to any rhythmic or melodic dictation is the ability to tap a beat at a steady tempo with the left hand while tapping divisions and subdivisions of the beat with the right.

1. Tap exercises (similar to the three given below) using whole, half, and quarter notes for the left hand beat while the right hand taps divisions of two or subdivisions of four of this beat. Prepare each drill by first establishing a steady tempo (approximately M.M. = 60) with the left hand.

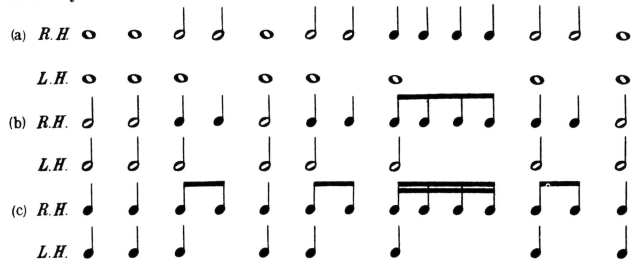

2. Tap exercises (similar to the three given below) using dotted whole, dotted half, and dotted quarter notes for the left hand beat while the right hand taps divisions of three or subdivisions of six of this beat.

Keyboard Drill.

1. Review Lesson 3.

Instructional Note:

Unit Three should be started at this time and should parallel the drill on the following exercises on duration. It is also suggested that this study of duration and tonality, which should proceed slowly due to the inability of the ear to assimilate this material readily, should be supplemented with a great deal of drill on sight singing and melodic dictation. The material used for this drill should parallel the following lessons.

Lesson 5.   The Bar Line;   The Measure.

Most melodies have a regular pattern regarding the accentuation of beats. Those patterns most commonly used are:

$$>U \quad >>U \quad and \quad >U>U$$

where   > = a primary accent,

                          > = a secondary accent, and

                          U = an unaccented beat.

Thus a melody such as America seems to require an accentuation as in Ex. 19.

Ex.19

This melody divides itself logically into groups of three quarter notes (or their equivalent). Therefore, for visual accommodation, a vertical line (called a measure bar, or bar line) is placed on the staff directly before each accented note. This triple grouping is thereby organized into groups of three quarter notes, with the primary accents falling on the first beat in the measure[1].

Ex. 20

The double bar (Ex. 20) is used at the end of a composition or exercise. It is also used within a composition to show the end of a section or movement, or whenever a change in measure or key signature occurs.

Ear Training.

1. Continue the drill of Lesson 4.

2. Listen to familiar melodies. Tap the beat with the left hand and the divisions with the right hand.

Keyboard Drill.

1. Play familiar melodies by ear. Begin the melodies on several different notes. For example: Play Row, Row, Row Your Boat beginning on C. When this can be played accurately play it beginning on F. Repeat this procedure starting on G, A, B, etc.

---

[1]A measure is the space between two successive measure bars.

Drill problems for Lesson 5 appear on Page 59

Lesson 6. The Time (or Measure) Signature; Classification.

In addition to adding measure bars, it is customary to indicate the grouping of beats by numbers (in the form of fractions) at the beginning of a composition. This is called the Time (or Measure) Signature.

Time Classification.

All time is classified as follows:

A. According to the number of beats in a measure, time is said to be
   1. Duple -----------------------------Two beats in each measure.
   2. Triple ----------------------------Three beats in each measure.
   3. Quadruple --------------------------Four beats in each measure.
   4. Quintuple -------------------------Five beats in each measure.
   5. Septuple --------------------------Seven beats in each measure.

B. According to the way these beats are normally divided, time is said to be
   1. Simple ---The regular division of the unit into two, or multiples of two. The numerator of the time signature shows the number of units in the measure. (This will be 2, 3, 4, 5, or 7.) The value of the unit is indicated by the denominator. (For example, the time signature 3/4 indicates that there are three beats in each measure, and the unit is a quarter note.)

   2. Compound -The regular division of the unit into three, or multiples of three. The numerator of the time signature will be 6, 9, or 12, but the number of units in the measure will be the numerator divided by 3. The value of the unit cannot be directly deduced from the denominator, as was the case in simple time. However, it will always be a dotted note, and equivalent to three of the notes indicated by the denominator. (For example, the time signature 6/8 implies two beats in each measure with a dotted quarter note unit.)

Time is therefore said to be "duple-simple", "triple-simple", "duple-compound", etc., depending upon the number of units in the measure and the way the unit is normally divided.

Example of Duple-Simple
Ex.21

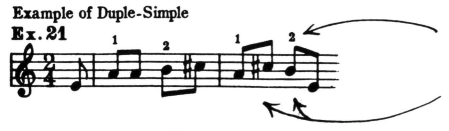

Two beats per measure. The unit is a quarter note.

The normal division of the unit is in twos.

Example of Duple-Compound
Ex.22

Two beats per measure. The unit is a dotted quarter note.

The normal division of the unit is in threes.

Drill problems for Lesson 6 appear on Page 61

The Classification of All Time Signatures.

Ex.23

Unit Division	Number of beats in measure	Duple 2	Triple 3	Quadruple 4	Quintuple 5	Septuple 7
S I M P L E	Signature	2 2 2 2 2 4 8 16	3 3 3 3 2 4 8 16	4 4 4 4 2 4 8 16	5 5 5 5 2 4 8 16	7 7 7 7 2 4 8 16
	Unit	𝅝 𝅗𝅥 ♪ ♪♪	𝅝 𝅗𝅥 ♪ ♪♪	𝅝 𝅗𝅥 ♪ ♪♪	𝅝 𝅗𝅥 ♪ ♪♪	𝅝 𝅗𝅥 ♪ ♪♪
C O M P O U N D	Signature	6 6 6 6 2 4 8 16	9 9 9 9 2 4 8 16	12 12 12 12 2 4 8 16		
	Unit	𝅝. 𝅗𝅥. ♩. ♪.	𝅝. 𝅗𝅥. ♩. ♪.	𝅝. 𝅗𝅥. ♩. ♪.		

Classification Not Affected by Tempo.

Regardless of the tempo, the classification remains unchanged. For example: A piece in 2/4 may be played so slowly that the beat does not coincide with the unit. In this case the beat would be the eighth note, but the unit would always remain the quarter, and the classification would still be Duple-Simple. (There are numerous examples of music in which the beat and unit do not coincide but it is best to avoid these in elementary dictation.)

Counting.

In instrumental music it is usually considered advisable, when first learning a piece, to count the beats in the measure. These numbers are shown above the notes in Ex. 24. When the unit is divided, as it is on the second beat of the second measure, the counting is 1 2 and 3, the "2" being tied over from the preceding beat and therefore not re-struck. "And" is, by definition, half-way between successive beats -- here, half-way between beats "2" and "3".

Ex.24

---

[1]"Quadruple-Simple" is sometimes referred to as "Common Time", but more recently the term "Common Time" refers only to 4/4 (C).

[2]"Quintuple Simple" and "Septuple-Simple" are sometimes referred to as "Added Times", "Quintuple" being a combination of 2+3 or 3+2, and "Septuple-Simple" 3+4 or 4+3. From this point of view these times might logically be considered as an irregular type of "Duple-Compound".

Borrowed Divisions.

Note, on page 9 , that all undotted notes (𝅝, 𝅗𝅥, ♩, ♪) divide normally into multiples of two. A note which is undotted may however be divided irregularly, by the use of proper notation. For example, a quarter note may be divided into three eighth notes of equal duration by placing the number "3" above (or below) the group. This "triplet" is borrowed from the compound times and superimposed over a simple division.

Similarly, a dotted note (𝅝·, 𝅗𝅥·, ♩·, ♪·) which divides normally into multiples of three, may be irregularly divided into two, or four notes of equal duration. This "duplet" or "quadruplet" pattern is borrowed from the simple times and superimposed over a compound division.

The notation of these borrowed divisions and subdivisions is again best illustrated by the use of a chart. (Also included in the chart is the division of a unit into five equal parts. This division belongs to neither simple nor compound time, but is occasionally used in either.)

Ex.25

Eer Training.

1. Listen to the playing of familiar melodies. Determine the time classification of each.

   Suggestions:

   (a) Tap the beat with the left hand. (This will usually be the normal walking speed, or the conducting beat.)
   (b) Determine which beat is accented, thereby learning the first term in the time classification; that is, duple, triple, quadruple, etc.
   (c) While tapping the beat with the left hand decide, by tapping divisions with the right hand, if the unit is divided into twos or threes, thus learning the second term in the time classification; that is, simple or compound.

2. Drill on all time classifications by tapping and counting. For example:

                     Duple-Simple

   Count: 1   2   1   2   1   2   1   2   1   2   etc.

   Tap (R.H.): '

   Tap (L.H.): '   '   '   '   '   '   '   '   '   '

                     Triple-Simple

   Count: 1   2   3   1   2   3   1   2   3   1   etc.

   Tap (R.H.): ''' ''' ''' ''' ''' ''' ''' ''' ''' '''

   Tap (L.H.): '   '   '   '   '   '   '   '   '   '

3. Continue the drill of Lesson 4.

Keyboard Drill.

1. Play familiar melodies as in Lesson 5. (Count the time.)

Lesson 7. <u>More Complex Problems of Duration.</u>

The division and subdivision of the unit and borrowed divisions were presented in Lessons 4 and 6. Further problems of a more complex nature need to be presented at this time. The ear training paralleling this lesson should continue throughout the student's study of music theory.

<u>Ties Within the Division.</u>

1. <u>Simple Time.</u>

    The tying of notes within the division of the unit[1] in simple time only results in the return to the unit:

2. The tying of notes within the division of the unit in compound time results in two patterns:

<u>Ties Within the Subdivision.</u>

  1. <u>Simple Time.</u>

      The following patterns result from ties within the subdivision of the quarter note unit:

  2. <u>Compound Time.</u>

      The following patterns result from ties within the subdivision of the dotted quarter note unit:

---

[1]The examples in this lesson are illustrated with only the quarter and dotted quarter note units.

Drill problems for Lesson 7 appear on Page 63

*(The starred patterns are those most often found in music litera-
ture. Also a few of the patterns above will be seen to be identical with patterns previously studied -- the division, and ties
within the division.)

Ties Between Units.

This is one of the most simple of the duration problems. A few
examples will suffice to illustrate both simple and compound
times:

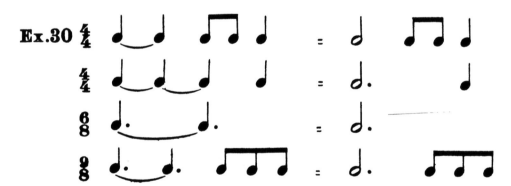

The tying of units to produce syncopation[1] is more complex.

[1]Syncopation results from the tying of a note on a weak beat into
one on a stronger beat.

Ties Between Divisions.

The tying between a unit and the next division, or between two divisions, results in still more complex patterns. Syncopation also occurs in some of these combinations.

Ex.31

Ties Between More Complex Patterns.

Ties between units which are irregular because of ties within the subdivision of the unit are difficult to execute as well as to hear in melodic and rhythmic dictation. The aural study of these should be reserved for more advanced study.

(Ex. 32)

Ex.32

Ear Training.

1. The patterns presented in this lesson should be drilled by tapping exercises and dictation until each can be recognized aurally. (This assumes that proficiency has been attained in less complex exercises.) In tapping the various patterns it is essential that the beat be maintained in the left hand. Examples:

2. Tap the rhythm of any melodies.
3. After drilling on exercises involving the quarter and dotted quarter note unit, the student should become familiar with the patterns based on the half or dotted half, and eighth and dotted eighth note unit. (This drill should be preceded by the writing out of the possible patterns with these units.)

Keyboard Drill.

1. Play familiar melodies with more complex rhythmic patterns.

Lesson 8. The Rest.

A "rest" is a symbol used in music to indicate the duration
of silence. Music would be very tiresome, both to the performer
and the listener, if there were continuous tones with no rests.

The value and the mathematical ratio of the rests correspond
to those of the notes.

Ex.33

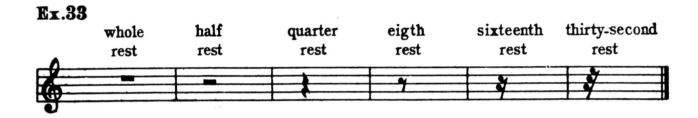

| whole rest | half rest | quarter rest | eigth rest | sixteenth rest | thirty-second rest |

A "whole rest" is generally used to indicate silence for an
entire measure regardless of the time signature.

Rests, like notes, may be dotted to increase their value by
one-half, but unlike notes, rests are never tied.

Ex.34

Drill problems for Lesson 8 appear on Page 65

UNIT THREE: TONALITY

Lesson 9. Basic Scales; The Major Scale.

Webster defines tonality as "the character which a composition has by virtue of its key, or through the relationship of its tones and chords to the keynote, or tonic". This relationship of tones is the result of organizing the seven notes (a b c d e f g -- either in their altered or unaltered form) into a prescribed pattern called a scale. The tonality is said to be that of the first and last note of the scale. This note is called the keynote, or tonic note.

The Seven Basic[1] Scales.

There are seven basic scales:

```
a b c d e f g a
  b c d e f g a b
    c d e f g a b c
      d e f g a b c d
        e f g a b c d e
          f g a b c d e f
            g a b c d e f g
```

Between each tone is found the interval[2] of either a half-step or a whole-step, but the distribution is different in each scale. (The half-steps are indicated by brackets.)

Previous to the 17th century the scales (or "modes" as they were usually called) in existence were primarily those basic scales shown above. Each had its own name:

a b c d e f g a -------------------------	Aeolian
b c d e f g a b -------------------------	Locrian
c d e f g a b c -------------------------	Ionian
d e f g a b c d -------------------------	Dorian
e f g a b c d e -------------------------	Phrygian
f g a b c d e f -------------------------	Lydian
g a b c d e f g -------------------------	Mixolydian

These scales were gradually altered (by the continued use of accidentals) until they lost their original tonality and were transformed into scales with which we are the most familiar today -- the major and the minor scales.

---

[1] The term "basic" as used throughout this workbook, refers to notation in its fundamental state, that is, unaltered.

[2] An interval is the pitch difference between two tones (or the alphabetical distance between two notes).

Drill problems for Lesson 9 appear on Page 67

The Major Scale.

The major scale is a direct alphabetical succession of eight tones. The interval between the 1st and 2nd, 2nd and 3rd, 4th and 5th, 5th and 6th, and 6th and 7th scale degrees (notes) is a whole-step. The interval between the 3rd and 4th, and 7th and 8th scale degrees is a half-step. (The "Ionian" mode fits this pattern.)

Ex. 35 The C Major Scale

This is called the "C major scale" from the name of the note upon which it starts and ends. A composition which makes use of this scale is said to be "in the key of C major".

All of the seven basic scales may be transformed into major scales by the use of accidentals; however, the above order of whole and half-steps must be adhered to.

Ex. 36 The D Major Scale   Ex. 37 The D♭ Major Scale

Ear Training.

1. Listen to major scales and learn to identify them by ear.

2. Sing major scales starting on any given tone.

3. Write major scales on the staff in whole notes. Drill as follows:

 (a) Establish the tonality by first playing the scale.
 (b) Point to various notes and sing the note to which you pointed.
 (c) Check your accuracy by occasionally playing the notes you sing.

4. Sing melodies based upon the major scale.

5. Use melodies in major keys for melodic dictation.

Keyboard Drill.

1. Continue drill of Lesson 5.

2. Spell and play all major scales (ascending and descending).
   The following procedure will facilitate the playing of
   scales for the beginning student:

   (a) The major scale is composed of two tetrachords[1]. The lower
       tetrachord is constructed the same as the upper. The two
       are joined by a whole-step. This is illustrated in Ex. 38.

Ex.38 The D Major Scale

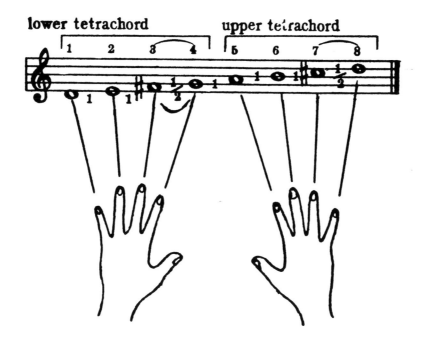

---

[1]A tetrachord is a diatonic series of four tones. Scale degrees
1, 2, 3, and 4 are called the lower tetrachord; 5, 6, 7, and 8
the upper tetrachord.

Lesson 10, Key Signatures (Major Tonality).

America, a part of which is shown in Example 20, is in the
key of G major. (The notes used in this melody are those found
only in the G major scale. Also the final note of America is
"G".) Since this melody is written in the key of G major, it is
necessary to place a sharp before every "F". To avoid this continued use of a sharp before each "F", the sharp is placed on the
fifth line just after the clef sign and before the time signature.
Every "F" occurring in the composition will then be played as an
"F sharp" unless indicated otherwise by an accidental.

Ex.39

The use of a key signature[1] is the usual procedure in writing
music in this period of traditional harmony. The sharps or flats
used in the key are grouped together and placed immediately after
the clef sign in a certain specified order. (See the following
page.)

Note on Accidentals.

Tones foreign to the key are often found in music. These
tones assume a character of secondary importance and have no direct
bearing upon the tonality. Ex. 40, below, is in the key of B♭ major.

Ex.40

"E natural"   "G flat" "G natural"

Any accidental placed before a note affects not only that
note but all other notes on that line or space throughout the
measure (Ex. 40). In the example above, note that the "G flat"
in the third measure has been tied into the "G flat" of the next
measure. The second "G" in the fourth measure, however, becomes
a "G natural". It would be wise here, for the sake of accurate
performance, to place a "precautionary accidental" (a natural
sign in this case) before this second "G" in the fourth measure.

---

[1]The key signature is "the sign composed of one or more sharps or
flats, placed after the clef at the beginning of a staff to desig-
nate the key".-Webster

Drill problems for Lesson 10 appear on Page 69

The key signatures for all major keys should be memorized. Learn the number of sharps or flats in the signature and their order and place upon the staff.

Aids for Learning the Major Key Signatures.

1. (a) If one begins with the key of C and progresses through one sharp, two sharps, three sharps, etc., each new key will begin on the 5th scale degree of the former key.

    (b) If one begins with the key of C and progresses through one flat, two flats, three flats, etc., each new key will begin on the 4th scale degree of the former key.

    This is best illustrated by the circle of fifths.

Ex.41 The Circle of Fifths

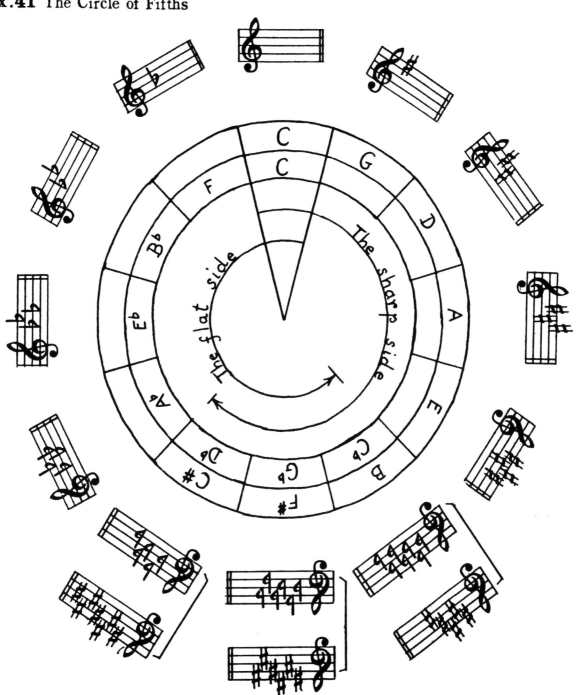

3. Notice in Ex. 41 that in the sharp keys (keys whose signatures contain sharps) that each new sharp is added to the preceding signature and is the sharped fourth scale degree of the preceding scale. It is the 7th scale degree of its own scale.

4. In the flat keys each new flat is also added to the preceding signature but is the 7th scale degree of the preceding scale and the 4th scale degree of its own.

5. Each sharp added is a perfect fifth <u>above</u> (or a perfect fourth below) the last.

6. Each flat added is a perfect fifth <u>below</u> (or a perfect fourth above) the last.

<u>In determining the key from the signature</u>:

   (a) The major key is a half-step above the last sharp in the signature, or
   (b) The major key is identical in name with the next to the last flat in the signature.

<u>Note</u>:   In writing key signatures, care should be taken to write the sharps or flats in the proper order on the staff. Also place them on the proper line or space. <u>Do not crowd!</u>

Ear Training.

1. Continue drill of Lesson 9.

2. While playing familiar melodies at the keyboard, stop at various places in the melody and hum the tonic note. (Check by playing the tonic note on the piano.)

Keyboard Drill.

1. Continue drill of Lessons 5 and 9.

Lesson 11. Minor Scales.

The minor scales are also a direct alphabetical succession of eight tones. The intervalic relationship between these tones, however, differs from that of the major scale.

A minor key has no signature of its own but borrows the key signature from the **major** key which is the most closely related.

Relative Keys.

The scale of "C major" - - c d e f g a b c - - differs only from the "A minor" scale - -a b c d e f g a- - in its tonic note (Ex. 42).

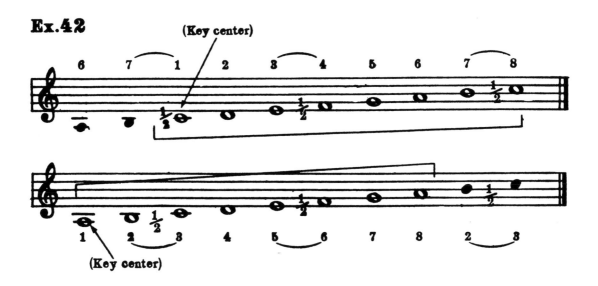

Ex. 42

The key of "A minor" is said to be the relative minor of "C major". Similarly the key of "C major" is the relative major of "A minor".

The tonic note of every minor key is 1½ steps below the tonic note of its related major. (It is identical with the 6th scale degree of its related major.) Thus the "G minor" scale is related to "B♭ major" and uses the key signature of "B♭ major".

Ex. 43 The "G minor" Scale

Drill problems for Lesson 11 appear on Page 71

The Three Forms of Minor - - Pure; Harmonic; and Melodic.

The minor scales previously explained (Exs. 42 and 43) are those whose tones follow exactly the key signature of their relative major. This form is called pure minor (normal minor, or aeolian minor).

Ex.44 The "C minor" Scale (Pure form)

Often, due to harmonic principles (which are studied in harmony), the 7th scale degree is raised a half-step. This form of minor is called harmonic minor.

Ex.45 The "C minor" Scale (Harmonic form)

The awkward 1½ step interval between scale degrees 6 and 7 in the harmonic minor scale is usually avoided in melodic writing by the following alterations of the pure form of the minor scale:

(a) In ascending, the 6th and 7th scale degrees are raised a half-step.

(b) In descending, the 6th and 7th scale degrees return to the pure form.

This scale is called the melodic minor.

Ex. 46 The "C minor" Scale (Melodic form)

Parallel Keys.

Scales which have the same tonic notes but are different in mode are said to be parallel, or homotonic. For example, "E minor" is parallel to "E major", but is relative to "G major".

Ear Training.

1. Listen to the three forms of minor scales and learn to identify them by ear.

2. Sing minor scales (three forms) starting on any given tone.

3. Drill on minor tonality as outlined in Lesson 9 (Ear Training No. 3).

4. Sing melodies based upon the minor scales.

5. Use melodies in minor keys for melodic dictation.

Keyboard Drill.

1. Spell and play the pure minor scale (ascending and descending), beginning on every note. (Follow the tetrachord system outlined in Lesson 9, page 23, making necessary intervalic adjustments.)

2. Spell and play the harmonic minor scale (ascending and descending), beginning on every note.

3. Spell and play the melodic minor scale (ascending and descending), beginning on every note.

UNIT FOUR: CHORD STRUCTURE

Lesson 12. Basic Triads.

Three or more tones may be combined to form a chord. The choice of such tones is primarily dictated by aesthetics; however, our sense of taste is strongly influenced by the harmony of the 18th and 19th century. Chords of this period were built upon the tertian system -- a system which builds chords in thirds[1].

By taking every other note in the basic scale alphabet (a b c d e f g) we arrive at the basic chord alphabet:

            a   c   e   g   b   d   f

The combining of all three adjacent tones in the chord alphabet results in the following seven basic triads[2]:

        ace   ceg   egb   gbd   bdf   dfa   fac

These basic triads, with the exception of "bdf", can be considered as being the 1st, 3rd, and 5th scale degrees of a major or minor scale. Those which fit the 1-3-5 pattern of the major scale are known as major triads, and those which fit the 1-3-5 pattern of the minor scales are known as minor triads. The "bdf" triad is called a diminished triad. (This triad is explained in Lesson 15.)

The seven basic triads are thereby classified as follows:

Ex. 47

Major	Minor	Diminished
fac ceg gbd	dfa ace egb	bdf

A fourth type of triad, the augmented triad, does not occur as one of the basic triads. (This triad is explained in Lesson 16.)

---

[1]The interval of a third occurs between any two adjacent notes in the basic chord alphabet, irrespective of chromatic inflection. For example: C up to E; C up to E♭ ; C♯ up to E; etc.

[2]A triad is a chord consisting of three different tones.

Drill problems for Lesson 12 appear on Page 75

Ear Training.

1. Continue drill on the past exercises.

2. Ear Training on triads is deferred until Lesson 13.

Keyboard Drill.

1. Spell and play the three basic major triads. For the present
    play all triads with the right hand -- thumb on the root, 3rd
    finger on the 3rd, and the 5th finger on the 5th. (See Ex. 49.)

    For example: Play an F major triad.

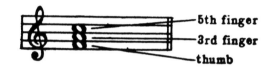

2. Spell and play the three basic minor triads.

3. Spell and play the one basic diminished triad.

Instructional Note:

        In Lessons 13 through 16 the four triad types are presented.
If the study of ear training is correlated with the written work
it is essential to drill on each type triad until it can be heard
in any position or inversion before proceeding to the next.

        Progress from this point on will be tedious and slow due
to the drill necessary for the aural assimilation of each triad
type. It will, therefore, probably be desirable to take up
Lessons 17, 18 and 19 during the aural study of Lesson 13.

Lesson 13. The Major Triad.

Each of the seven basic triads may be transformed into a major triad by chromatic alteration. Ex. 48 shows the possibilities with the basic triad "dfa". (The root of the chord has not been double flatted or double sharped.)

Ex. 48

D Major   Db Major   D# Major

Preliminary Method for Spelling the Major Triad[1].

In spelling major triads think the 1st, 3rd, and 5th scale degrees of a major scale. For example: Spell an "Ab major" triad. Think the Ab major scale and write down the 1st, 3rd, and 5th of the scale thus: ab c   eb .

This in turn may be transferred to the staff:

Ex. 49

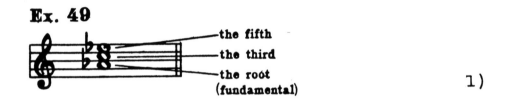

the fifth
the third
the root
(fundamental)

1)

The components of a triad are named as in Ex. 49. This triad is called an "Ab major" triad. The chord's name is derived from the root of the chord. Any order or combination of the tones ab c   eb constitutes an "Ab major" triad. The following are all "Ab major" triads. (The numbers indicate the triad component.)

Ex. 50

---

[1]Other methods of chord spelling will suggest themselves after the study of intervals.

Drill problems for Lesson 13 appear on Page 77

Ear Training.

1. Sing a major triad considering any given tone as the root.
   Example: Given "G" as the root of a major triad:

Play	Sing	Check by playing
	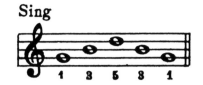	

2. When Exercise 1 is mastered sing a major triad considering any tone as the 5th. Example: Given "C" as the 5th of a major triad:

Play	Sing	Check by playing

3. When Exercises 1 and 2 are mastered sing a major triad considering any tone as the 3rd. Example: Given "G" as the 3rd of a major triad:

Play	Sing	Check by playing

4. Instructor plays major chords in all positions[1] and inversions[2]. Student indicates he has heard a major triad by writing a capital "M". The number placed above the "M" refers to the top part (soprano), and the number placed below the "M" refers to the lowest part (bass). For example:

Instructor plays:

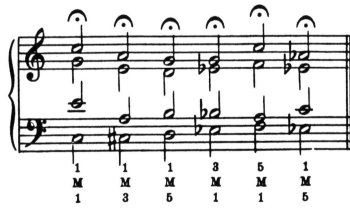

Student writes:

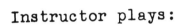

---

[1] Position of the octave = root in the soprano
Position of the third = 3rd in the soprano
Position of the fifth = 5th in the soprano

[2] Root position = root in the bass
1st inversion = 3rd in the bass
2nd inversion = 5th in the bass

5. Begin only after Exercises 1-4 have been mastered.

Instructor announces a tone which is to be played in the soprano. He plays a major triad with the given tone in the soprano. Student hears given tone as 1, 3, or 5 and thereby spells the triad that was played by the instructor. For example: Given tone: "A" in the soprano.

Instructor plays:

Student writes down given note. He listens for the soprano which will sound 1, 3, or 5 -- that is, it will fit into one of the patterns of Exercises 1, 2, or 3 above. Student spells chord.

Student writes: a^5- d f♯ a

6. Sing major melodies built primarily on major triad structure.

7. Use major melodies built primarily on major triad structure for melodic dictation.

Keyboard Drill.

1. Spell and play major triads with any given tone as 1, 3, or 5. For example: Play a major triad whose 3rd is "G". Play: e♭ g b♭ .

Instructional Note.

The study of part-writing, harmony and harmonic dictation may be introduced at this time if it is desired. However, this study should be limited to the major triads until the others have been introduced as isolated chord types.

Also, if this work is introduced, the keyboard exercises become much more complex. In this case they would parallel the written work in harmony. (Suggested drill: Figured basses, melody harmonization, harmonic progressions, transposition, score reading, modulation, etc.)

Lesson 14. The <u>Minor</u> <u>Triad</u>.

Each of the seven basic triads may be transformed into a
<u>minor</u> triad by chromatic alteration.   Ex. 51 shows the possi-
bilities with the basic triad "dfa".

Ex.51

Already D Minor Dｂ Minor D♯Minor

<u>Preliminary</u> <u>Method</u> <u>for</u> <u>Spelling</u> <u>the</u> <u>Minor</u> <u>Triad</u>.

In spelling minor triads think the 1st, 3rd, and 5th scale
degrees of a <u>minor</u> scale. For example: Spell an "F minor"
triad. Think the "F minor" scale and write down the 1st, 3rd,
and 5th of the scale thus: f aｂ c .

<u>Ear</u> <u>Training</u>.

1. Follow the presentation of Ear Training Exercises 1-7, Lesson 13.
    Major and minor triads may now be mixed in aural drill exercises.

<u>Keyboard</u> <u>Drill</u>.

1. Spell and play minor triads with any given tone as 1, 3, or 5.

<u>Instructional</u> <u>Note</u>:

The minor triad may now be added if part-writing, harmony,
and harmonic dictation were introduced after Lesson 13. But
first, skill should be acquired in aural recognition of the isolated
minor triad in all positions and inversions.

Drill problems for Lesson 14 appear on Page 79

Lesson 15. The Diminished Triad.

Each of the seven basic triads may be transformed into a diminished triad by chromatic alteration. Ex. 52 shows the possibilities with the basic triad "dfa".

Ex. 52

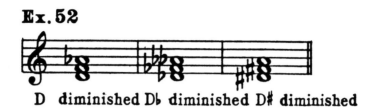

D diminished D♭ diminished D♯ diminished

Preliminary Method for Spelling the Diminished Triad.

In spelling diminished triads think a minor triad and then lower the 5th a half-step. For example: Spell an "A diminished" triad. Think the "A minor" triad -- a c e -- and lower the 5th a half-step: a c e♭

Ear Training.

1. Follow the presentation of Ear Training Exercises 1-7, Lesson 13. Major, minor, and diminished triads may now be mixed in aural drill exercises.

Keyboard Drill.

1. Spell and play diminished triads with any given tone as 1, 3, or 5.

Instructional Note:

The importance of the diminished triad is considerably less than that of the major and minor triads. Therefore, time spent in drill should be proportionately decreased.

After skill has been acquired in aural recognition of the diminished triad, it may be introduced into the study of part-writing, harmony, and harmonic dictation.

Drill problems for Lesson 15 appear on Page 81

Lesson 16. The Augmented Triad.

Each of the seven basic triads may be transformed into an augmented triad by chromatic alteration. Ex. 53 shows the possibilities with the basic triad "fac".

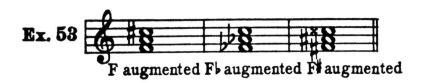

F augmented Fb augmented F♯ augmented

Preliminary Method for Spelling the Augmented Triad:

In spelling augmented triads think a major triad and raise the 5th a half-step. For example: Spell an "Ab Augmented" triad. Think the "Ab major" triad -- ab c eb-- and raise the 5th a half-step: ab c e♮

Ear Training.

1. Follow the presentation of Ear Training Exercises 1-7, Lesson 13. Major, minor, diminished, and augmented triads may now be mixed in aural drill exercises. The drill exercises on the augmented triad should be limited to chords in root position. Due to this equi-distant chord, it is impossible to hear inversions. In listening to soprano position, compare the soprano tone to that of the bass.

Keyboard Drill.

1. Spell and play augmented triads with any given tone as 1, 3, or 5.

Instructional Note:

Like the diminished triad, the augmented triad is less important than the major and minor. Time spent on drill exercises should be less.

After a certain amount of skill has been acquired in aural recognition of the augmented triad, it may be introduced into the study of part-writing, harmony, and harmonic dictation. But there, too, its use is limited.

Drill problems for Lesson 16 appear on Page 83

Lesson 17. Intervals.

As stated in the footnote on page 21, "An interval is the pitch difference between two tones (or the alphabetical distance between two notes)". The alphabetical distance between two notes first classifies intervals into primes, 2nds, 3rds, 4ths, 5ths, 6ths, 7ths, and octaves. Ex. 54 illustrates the naming of these basic intervals.

Ex. 54

| Primes (or unisons) | 2nds | 3rds | 4ths | 5ths | 6ths | 7ths | octaves |

The use of accidentals does not change the <u>basic</u> interval spelling. The following intervals are <u>all</u> 2nds:

Ex. 55

It is obvious that the above 2nds are not all alike.

Between f and g is a whole-step.
Between f and g♯ is a step-and-a-half.
Between f♯ and g♯ is a whole-step.
Between f𝄪 and g is a half-step.

Drill problems for Lesson 17 appear on Page 85

This discrepancy necessitates a further classification of intervals -- a classification dependent upon the number of whole-steps and half-steps involved. The terms perfect, major, minor, diminished, and augmented are used in the secondary classification.

Intervals Based Upon the Major Scale.

Only perfect and major intervals occur between the keynote and the other degrees of the major scale: (P = perfect; M = major; m = minor; d = diminished; A = augmented. Therefore, M 3 = major 3rd; P 4 = perfect 4th; etc.)

Ex. 56

1. In the major scale (Ex. 56) primes, 4ths, 5ths, and octaves are called perfect. If these intervals are chromatically altered to increase their size a half-step they become augmented. If they are chromatically altered to decrease their size a half-step they become diminished.

Ex. 57

Diminished 5th   Perfect 5th   Augmented 5th

(Since the spelling is basically "C" up to "G", the intervals must be classified as 5ths.)

2. In the major scale (Ex. 56) 2nds, 3rds, 6ths, and 7ths are called major. If these intervals are chromatically altered to increase their size a half-step they become augmented. If they are chromatically altered to decrease their size a half-step they become minor. If their size is further decreased a half-step they become diminished.

Ex. 58

Minor 6th   Major 6th   Augmented 6th

Diminished intervals are normally limited to 4ths, 5ths, 7ths, and occasionally 3rds. Augmented intervals are limited to 2nds, 4ths, 5ths, and occasionally 6ths. Avoid writing intervals that are enharmonic with perfect intervals.)

Note: Perfect intervals never become major or minor intervals.
        Neither do major nor minor intervals become perfect.

The above is diagramed in Ex. 59.

Ex. 59

Diminished ←	——→ Perfect ← (Primes, 4ths, 5ths, octaves)	→ Augmented
Diminished ←	→ Minor ← → Major ← (2nds, 3rds, 6th, 7ths)	→ Augmented

increase in size by half-steps ⟶

⟵ decrease in size by half-steps

Intervals may be melodic or harmonic.

Ex. 60 Melodic Intervals

Ex. 61 Harmonic Intervals

Inversion of Intervals -- Two Rules.

1. Primes invert to octaves -- octaves invert to primes:

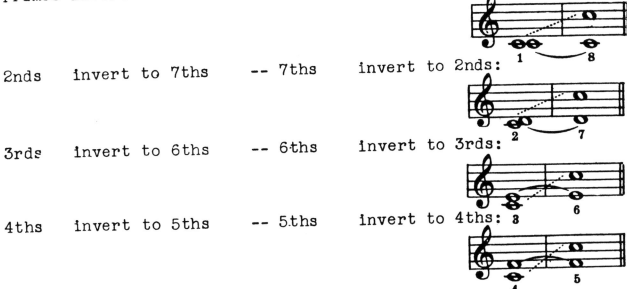

    2nds   invert to 7ths   -- 7ths   invert to 2nds:

    3rds   invert to 6ths   -- 6ths   invert to 3rds:

    4ths   invert to 5ths   -- 5ths   invert to 4ths:

2. Perfect intervals invert to perfect intervals:

    Major intervals invert to minor intervals --
    Minor intervals invert to major intervals:

    Augmented intervals invert to diminished intervals
    Diminished intervals invert to augmented intervals:

Examples of the Way the Two Rules Combine:

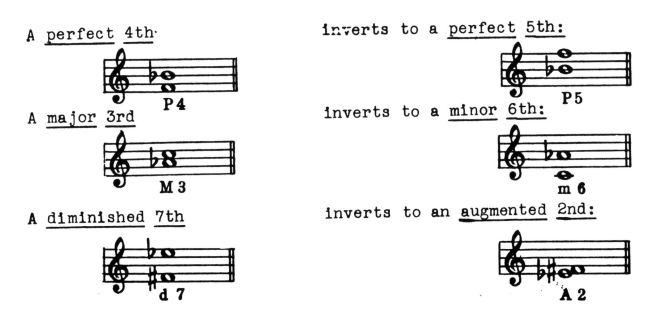

A perfect 4th   inverts to a perfect 5th:

P4   P5

A major 3rd   inverts to a minor 6th:

M3   m 6

A diminished 7th   inverts to an augmented 2nd:

d 7   A 2

Ear Training.

1. Learn to identify the various isolated intervals by the following methods:

(a) The octave -- Strike a note on the piano. Sing first that tone then the octave above or below.

(b) The major third -- From any given tone sing a major third above by thinking 1 up to 3 in a major triad. Sing a major third below by thinking 3 down to 1 in a major triad.

(c) The perfect fifth -- From any given tone sing a perfect fifth above by thinking 1 up to 5 in a major triad. Sing a perfect fifth below by thinking 5 down to 1 in a major triad.

(d) The minor third -- From any given tone sing a minor third above by thinking 1 up to 3 in a minor triad. Sing a minor third below by thinking 3 down to 1 in a minor triad.

(e) The augmented fifth -- From any given tone sing an augmented fifth above by thinking 1 up to 5 in an augmented triad.

(f) The diminished fifth -- From any given tone sing a diminished fifth above by thinking 1 up to 5 in a diminished triad. Sing a diminished fifth below by thinking 5 down to 1 in a diminished triad.

(g) The perfect fourth, major and minor sixth, and major and minor seventh can best be learned by studying them as they relate to the scale. Refer again to the Ear Training Exercise 3, Lesson 9.

2. In tonal thinking (that is, for those intervals which contain tones in the major or minor scale), it is helpful to be familiar with the various degrees of activity of the scale degrees. For example: the 2nd scale degree wants to move to the root (sometimes to the 3rd); the 4th to the 3rd; the 6th to the 5th; and the 7th to the octave.

3. For those intervals which contain altered tones, in major or minor tonality, it is helpful to consider such altered tones as being non-harmonic. Listen to the implied resolution.

Keyboard Drill.

1. Play familiar melodies whose introductory motives are based on the above intervals.

2. Play basic intervals above and below any given white note on the piano. Play first as a melodic then as a harmonic interval.

3. Play the following intervals above and below any given note: P 1, M 2, M 3, P 4, M 6, M 7, P 8. (Refer again to Ex. 56).

4. Play any interval above any given note. (Use the method suggested in Ex. 56, p. 39, making any necessary adjustments -- decreasing or increasing the size of the interval -- when a minor, diminished, or augmented interval is desired.)

Lesson 18. Inversion of Triads; Figured Bass.

A triad with its root in the lowest part is said to be in root position; with the chord third in the lowest part it is in first inversion; and with the chord fifth in the lowest part in second inversion.

Ex. 62

Root position   1st Inversion   2nd Inversion

A system of indicating the inversion of a chord, called "figured bass", is in general usage. This system indicates the intervals which occur from the bass (or lowest) part up to each of the above parts.

Ex. 63

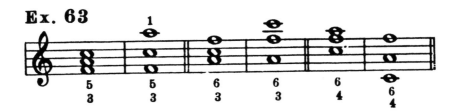

The figuring is usually reduced to its minimum essentials. No number is used if a triad is in root position; only a "6" if it is in 1st inversion; and the "6" if it is in 2nd inversion.
                                                  4

Ex. 64

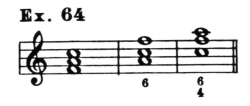

(A chord in 1st inversion is called a "chord of the sixth" and one in 2nd inversion a "six-four chord".)

[1] In this chord the interval from "F" up to "A" is the interval of a 10th, but more often it is called a "3rd" since it is an octave plus a "3rd". In this case it is known as a compound interval.

Drill problems for Lesson 18 appear on Page 87

The kinds of intervals which occur above the lowest part (3rds, 4ths, 5ths, or 6ths) -- and therefore, the type chord -- are dictated by the key signature.

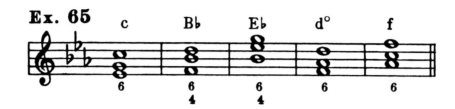

Alterations can be indicated in this system by placing the appropriate accidental before the number representing the altered note.

It will be noted in Ex. 66 that (a) partial or complete figuring is often necessary to indicate the alteration, (b) an accidental standing alone refers to the third above the lowest part; for example: ♭ = ♭3; ♯ = ♯3, and (c) any alteration of the lowest part need not be indicated since that part is always given in the "figured bass". Remember, in this system, that the figures refer to the interval above the lowest part.

Ear Training.

1. Continue drill of the exercises on triad recognition.

2. Continue drill on chord spelling from the soprano, Exercise 5, page 34. Indicate the inversion by use of "6" for 1st inversion, and "6" for 2nd. For example:
    4

$$a \ 3 \quad - \quad f \ a \ c \ {}^{6}_{4}$$

3. Continue drill on intervals.

Keyboard Drill.

1. Play major triads in first inversion. For example: Play a "G major" triad.

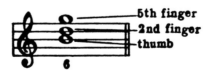

2. Play minor triads in first inversion. Finger as above.

3. Play diminished triads in first inversion. Finger as above.

4. Play major triads in second inversion. For Example: Play a "G major" triad:

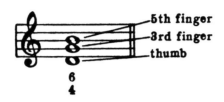

5. Play minor triads in second inversion. Finger as above.

6. Play diminished triads in second inversion. Finger as above.

7. Continue the following drill exercise chromatically through the octave. (Play with the right hand alone, using the fingering indicated in previous inversions.)

8. Play the above keyboard drill exercise (No. 7) with the left hand, an octave lower.

9. Play a sequence of minor triads, similar to Exercise 7 above, with the right hand.

10. Play a sequence of minor triads, similar to Exercise 7 above, with the left hand.

Lesson 19. Triads as Chords Within a Tonality.

The use of scales to establish a tonality was discussed in Lesson 9. Three triads (major or minor) with their roots a perfect fifth apart, will also establish a tonality, with the tonic note being identical with the root of the middle chord.

Ex. 67

Key of B♭ Major

Notice that the B♭ major scale may be derived directly from the notes of the above three triads:

b♭   c   d   e♭   f   g   a   b♭

The relationship between triads and scale degrees in establishing a tonality is obvious once the triad is considered as an expansion of the root tone. Each degree of the scale may be the root of a triad. The triad type is of course governed by the scale (key signature).[1]

Ex. 68

I   ii   iii   IV   V   vi   vii°   I

The triads above are numbered with Roman Numerals. Note that the triads built on scale degrees 1, 4, and 5 are major (labeled with large numerals -- I, IV, and V); those on scale degrees 2, 3, and 6 are minor (labeled with small numerals -- ii, iii and vi)   and the one on scale degree 7, diminished (labeled with a small numeral and a degree sign -- vii°). The augmented triad occurs on scale degree 3 (labeled III⁺) in the harmonic minor scale.

---

[1]The basic triads may be obtained by building triads above each note of the "C major" scale.

Drill problems for Lesson 19 appear on Page 89

The following example shows triads built on the scale of "E♭ major".

Ex. 69

I   ii   iii   IV   V   vi   vii°   I

Names have been assigned to the different chords that occur within a given tonality. This avoids the confusion that results from the over-use of numbers.

The I	is called the	TONIC	chord.
The ii	is called the	SUPERTONIC	chord.
The iii	is called the	MEDIANT	chord.
The IV	is called the	SUBDOMINANT	chord.
The V	is called the	DOMINANT	chord.
The vi	is called the	SUBMEDIANT	chord.
The vii°	is called the	LEADING TONE	chord.

It is the logical choice and function of these chords in music that constitues the study of <u>harmony</u>.

Ear Training.

1. At this point, or perhaps just after the study of the major triad, the student should concentrate on the study of <u>har- monic dictation</u>. The recognition of chords within a tonality and particularly the recognition and writing on the staff of chord patterns such as ii$_6$ V I; I IV V vi; etc., should be stressed. It is through the correlated study of harmony, ear training, sight singing, and keyboard that the student can best acquire musical literacy.

Keyboard Drill.

1. Play the tonic, subdominant, or dominant triads (in root posi- tion) in any given major key. For example: Play the dominant of B♭ major.

B♭: V

2. Play the tonic, subdominant, or dominant triad in any given minor key (harmonic form).

3. Play any triad (I, ii, iii, IV, V, vi, vii°) in any given major

4. Play any triad in any given minor key.

DRILL PROBLEMS

After solving each drill problem, the
student should play it on the piano.

Drill Problems

Lesson 1.

1. If "middle C" vibrates 256 v.p.s. how many times per second does the "C" an octave higher vibrate? _____

2. What would be the frequency of vibration of the "C" an octave below "middle C"? _____

3. What would be the frequency of the "C" two octaves above "middle C"? _____

4. Draw on the staff only that part of the treble clef that identifies "G".

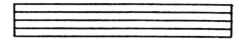

5. Draw that part of the bass clef that identifies "F".

6. Write the names under the following notes:

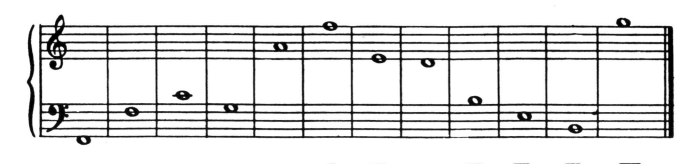

Name _____

Drill Problems

Lesson 2.

1. Rewrite the following notes in the bass clef so that they will sound the same. (Do not use the 8va sign.)

2. Rewrite the following notes in the treble clef so that they will sound the same. (Do not use the 8va sign.)

3. Transpose (write) the following notes an octave lower. (Do not use the 8va sign.)

4. Transpose the following notes an octave higher. (Do not use the 8va sign.)

5. Rewrite the following notes at the same pitch, using the 8va sign for those notes that go above the staff.

Name_____

Drill Problems

<u>Lesson 3.</u>

1. Write the following notes on the staff as indicated. (Remember that the accidental is placed <u>before</u> the note.)

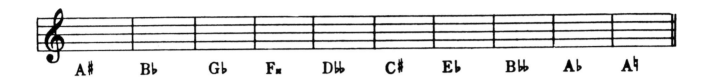

2. Write the names under the following notes. (Follow the example above.)

3. Write a chromatic scale, ascending and descending, starting on D.

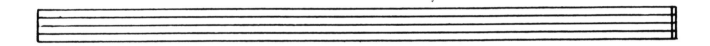

4. Write the enharmonic equivalents of the following notes. The first is solved as an example.

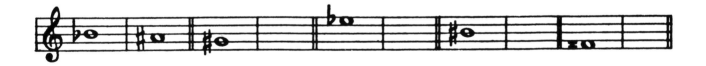

Name_____

Drill Problems

Lesson 4.

1. Write examples on the staff of all the different kinds of notes.
   Put flags on all notes of shorter duration than the quarter.

Note: If a note is below the 3rd line the stem is placed on the
right side of the note and turned up. If it is on or above the 3rd
line, the stem is placed on the left side of the note and turned down.

2. Connect the following groups of notes by the use of "bars"
   rather than "flags".

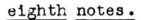

eighth notes.   sixteenth notes.

Note: The rule above cannot be rigidly followed when more than one
note is barred together. Turn all of the stems down if most of
the notes are above the middle line and up if most of the notes are
below.

3. Supply the number that correctly completes the following equations.

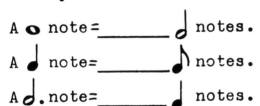   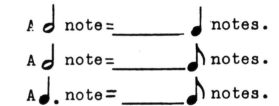

4. Rewrite the following tied notes using dots in place of ties.

5. Complete the following chart.

Unit	Division	Subdivision
♪		
♪.		

Name_____

Drill Problems.

<u>Lesson 5.</u>

1. Hum (or play) the following melodies. (1) Mark, with only the
   primary accents, those notes which seem to demand the most stress,
   and (2) place measure bars before each accented note.

(a)

(b)

(c)

(d)

Name _____

Drill Problems

Lesson 6.

1. Complete the following chart. The first is solved as an
   example.

Time Signature	$\frac{4}{4}$	$\frac{2}{4}$	$\frac{6}{8}$	$\frac{5}{4}$	$\frac{3}{2}$	$\frac{6}{4}$	$\frac{9}{8}$	$\frac{3}{8}$	$\frac{7}{8}$	$\frac{2}{2}$	$\frac{6}{16}$	$\frac{12}{4}$
Number beats in measure	4											
The Unit is	♩											
Time Classification	Q.-S.											

2. Write the correct time signature in each of the following
   measures:

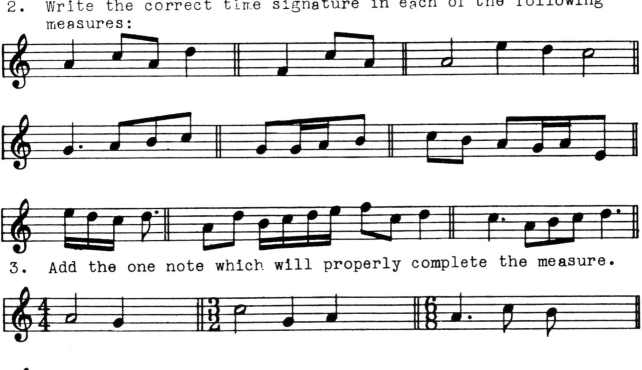

3. Add the one note which will properly complete the measure.

4. Fill in the following measures with appropriate notes.
   (Write melodic fragments similar to those in Exercise 2
   above.)

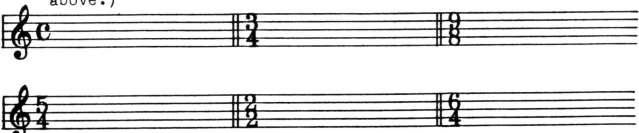

Name_____

Drill Problems

Lesson 7.

1. Write the correct time signatures in each of the following measures.

2. Add the one note which will properly complete the measure.

3. Fill in the following measures with appropriate notes. Use patterns discussed in this lesson.

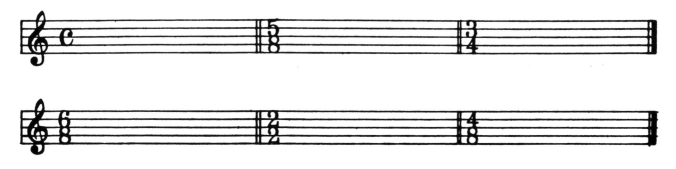

Name_____

DRILL PROBLEMS

Lesson 8.

1. Write several examples (on the staff) of all different kinds of rests.

Whole rests | **Half rests**

Quarter rests | **Eighth rests**

Sixteenth rests | **Thirty-second rests**

2. Write the correct time signature in each of the following measures.

3. Add the one rest which will properly complete each of the following measures.

4. Supply the number that correctly completes the following equations.

A 𝄻 rest= __________ 𝄽 rests. A 𝄼 rest= ________ 𝄾 rests.

A 𝄼 rest= __________ 𝄽 rests. A 𝄽 rest= ________ 𝄿 rests.

A 𝄽. rest= __________ 𝄾 rests. A 𝄾 rest= ________ 𝅀 rests.

Name ____________________

Lesson 9.

1. Write major scales (ascending and descending) as indicated.
   Do not use a key signature. The first is solved as an example.

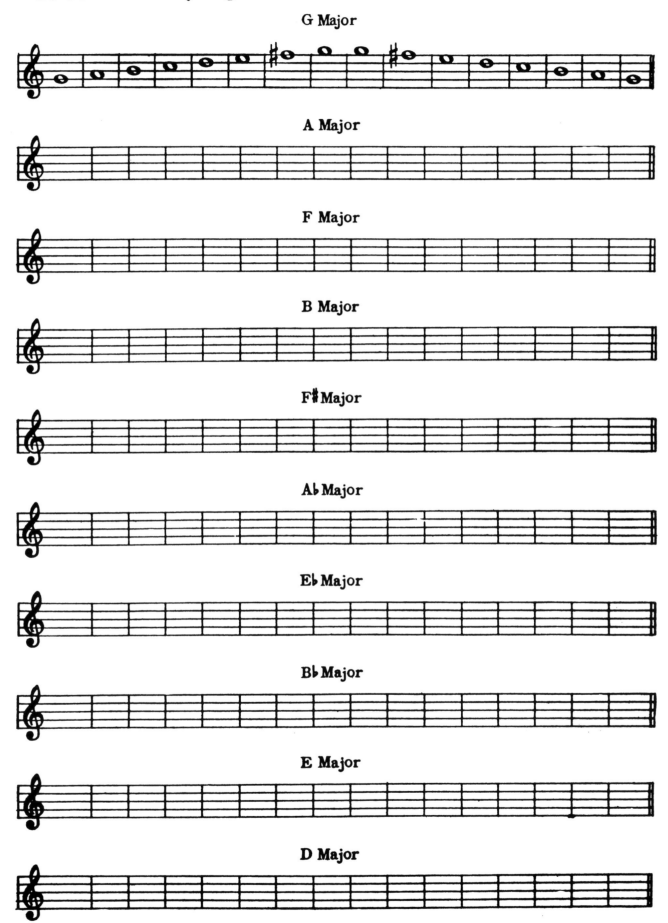

Drill Problems

1. Drill problem 1c, Lesson 5, is in the key of D major. Re-
    write this with the proper key and time signature.

2. Write the key signatures on the staff as indicated and the
    name of the major key below the staff. Use capital letters
    to indicate major tonality. The "pattern" of the key signa-
    ture is the same in the bass clef as it is in the treble.
    The first problem is solved as an example.

1 sharp	6 sharps	2 flats	5 flats	1 flat
G				

2 sharps	3 flats	5 sharps	7 sharps	7 flats

3. Write major scales (ascending and descending) as indicated.
    Use a key signature. Use the bass clef for the first five scales,
    and the treble clef for the remaining.

C Major

G Major

F Major

D Major

Bb Major

(cont'd.)   Name_____

70

Drill Problems, cont'd. (Lesson 10)

A Major

E♭ Major

E Major

A♭ Major

B Major

D♭ Major

F♯ Major

G♭ Major

C♯ Major

C♭ Major

Name _____

Drill Problems

Lesson 11.

1. In Ex. 41, page 25, the key signatures are given for all the major keys. Write below the staff the names of the minor keys which correspond to the signatures given, that is, the relative minor. (Use small letters to denote minor.)

2. Write the key signatures on the staff as indicated and the name of the minor key below the staff. Use small letters for minor keys. The first problem is solved as an example.

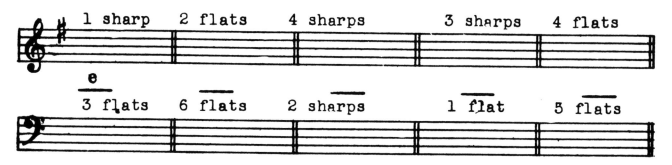

3. Write pure minor scales (ascending only) as indicated. Use a key signature. Use the treble clef.

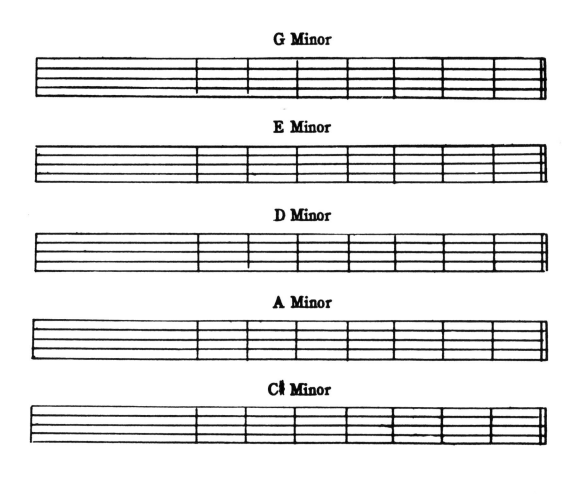

(Cont'd.)   Name_____

Drill Problems, cont'd. (Lesson 11)

4. Write harmonic minor scales (ascending only) as indicated. Use a key signature. Use the bass clef.

G Minor

C Minor

F Minor

E Minor

F# Minor

Bb Minor

C# Minor

B Minor

Eb Minor

(Cont'd.)   Name_____

Drill Problems, cont'd. (Lesson 11)

5. Write melodic minor scales (ascending and descending) as
   indicated. Use a key signature.

A Minor

D Minor

F Minor

E Minor

C# Minor

Eb Minor

F# Minor

G Minor

Name_____

Drill Problems

Lesson 12.

1. Spell basic triads considering the given note as indicated.
   The first exercise is solved as an example.

Given	Root	3rd	5th
c	*c e g*	*a c e*	*f a c*
e			
g			
b			
d			
f			
a			

2. Spell the three basic triads that are major.

   (a) _____ (b) _____ (c) _____

3. Spell the three basic triads that are minor.

   (a) _____ (b) _____ (c) _____

4. Spell the one diminished basic triad. _____

5. Does the augmented triad occur as a basic triad? _____

   Name _____

Drill Problems

Lesson 13.

1. Spell major triads. Consider the following given notes as 1, 3, and 5. The first is solved as an example.

Given	Root	3rd	5th
c	*c e g*	*ab c eb*	*f a c*
d			
g			
b			
f#			
eb			
f			

2. Write major triads on the staff. Consider the following given notes as the fundamental. The first is solved as an example.

given

3. Write major triads. Consider the following given notes as the third. The first is solved as an example.

given

4. Write major triads. Consider the following given notes as the fifth. The first is solved as an example.

given

Name_____

Drill Problems

Lesson 14.

1. Spell minor triads. Consider the following given notes as 1, 3, and 5. The first is solved as an example.

Given	Root	3rd	5th
c	*c eb g*	*a c e*	*f ab c*
f			
g			
a			
bb			
f#			
e			

2. Write minor triads. Consider the following given notes as the fundamental. The first is solved as an example.

3. Write minor triads. Consider the following given notes as the third. The first is solved as an example.

4. Write minor triads. Consider the following given notes as the fifth. The first is solved as an example.

Name_____

Drill Problems

Lesson 15.

1. Spell diminished triads. Consider the following given notes as 1, 3, and 5. The first is solved as an example.

Given	Root	3rd	5th
c	c eb gb	a c eb	f♯ a c
d			
e			
g			
bb			
g♯			
b			

2. Write diminished triads. Consider the following given notes as the fundamental. The first is solved as an example.

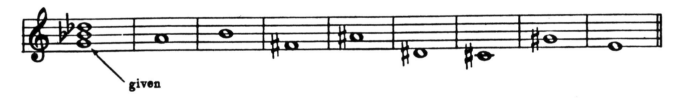

3. Write diminished triads. Consider the following given notes as the third. The first is solved as an example.

4. Write diminished triads. Consider the following given notes as the fifth. The first is solved as an example.

Name_____

Drill Problems

Lesson 16.

1. Spell augmented triads. Consider the following given notes as 1, 3, and 5. The first is solved as an example.

Given	Root	3rd	5th
d	*d f♯ a♯*	*b♭ d f♯*	*g♭ b♭ d*
e			
c			
d♭			
a			
b♭			
f			

2. Write augmented triads. Consider the following given notes as the fundamental. The first is solved as an example.

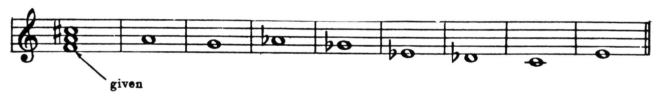

3. Write augmented triads. Consider the following given notes as the third. The first is solved as an example.

4. Write augmented triads. Consider the following given notes as the fifth. The first is solved as an example.

(cont'd.)   Name _____

Drill Problems, cont'd. (Lesson 16)

5. Name the following triads. Use the abbreviations:

    Major triad: Capital letter. (Example: F; B♭ ; etc.)
    Minor triad: Small letter. (Example: f; b♭ ; etc.)
    Diminished triad: Small letter with degree sign.
    (Example: f° ; b° ; etc.)
    Augmented triads: Capital letter with plus sign.
    (Example: F⁺ ; B♭⁺; etc.)

    The first is solved as an example.

F#　___　___　___　___　___　___

___　___　___　___　___　___

6. Spell the triads indicated. Consider the following given
    notes as the fundamental (root).

Given as 1	Major	Minor	Diminished	Augmented
c				
d				
f#				
g				
e				
a♭				
d♭				
e♭				
b♭				

Name_____

Drill Problems

Lesson 17.

1. Write basic intervals above each note as indicated. The first two are solved as an example.

2. Name the following intervals and classify as to type. The first is solved as an example.

3. Write harmonic intervals <u>above</u> each note as indicated. The first is solved as an example.

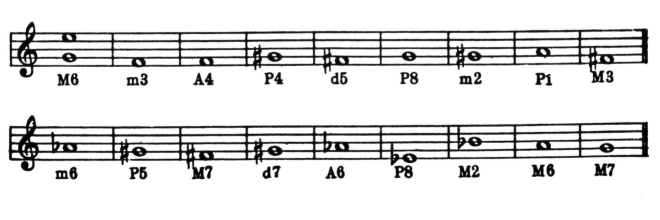

(cont'd.)   Name_____

Drill Problems, cont'd. (Lesson 17)

4. Write harmonic intervals below each note as indicated. The first is solved as an example.

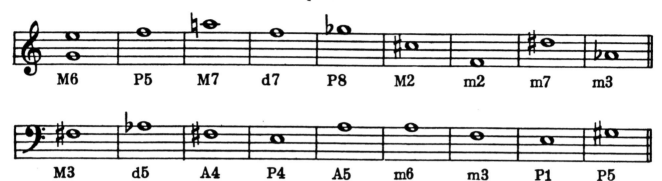

5. In a major scale, what is the interval from 1 up to 5? _____;
   1 up to 3? _____; 1 up to 6? _____

6. In a harmonic minor scale what is the interval from 1 up to
   5? _____; 1 up to 3? _____; 1 up to 6? _____

7. Complete the following statements:

   (a) A P 5 inverts to a _____.   (f) A d 7 inverts to a____.
   (b) A M 3 inverts to a _____.   (g) A M 7 inverts to a____.
   (c) A m 7 inverts to a _____.   (h) A M 2 inverts to a____.
   (d) A d 5 inverts to a _____.   (i) A m 2 inverts to a____.
   (e) A m 3 inverts to a _____.   (j) A P 4 inverts to a____.

8. Complete the following statements:

   (a) An A 4 is enharmonic with a _____.
   (b) An A 5 is enharmonic with a _____.
   (c) A m 3 is enharmonic with a _____.
   (d) A d 5 is enharmonic with a _____.
   (e) A m 7 is enharmonic with a _____.

9. Complete the following statements:

   (a) In the major triad the interval from 1 up to 3 is a _____.
   (b) In the major triad the interval from 1 up to 5 is a _____.
   (c) In the major triad the interval from 3 up to 5 is a _____.
   (d) In the minor triad the interval from 1 up to 3 is a _____.
   (e) In the minor triad the interval from 1 up to 5 is a _____.
   (f) In the minor triad the interval from 3 up to 5 is a _____.
   (g) In the aug. triad the interval from 1 up to 5 is an _____.
   (h) In the dim. triad the interval from 1 up to 5 is a _____.

Name_____

Drill Problems

Lesson 18.

1. Write the following triads <u>in first inversion</u> on the staff.
   The first is solved as an example.

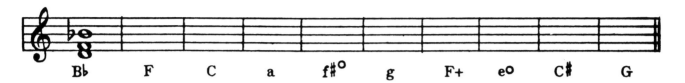

Bb   F   C   a   f#°   g   F+   e°   C#   G

2. Write the following triads <u>in second inversion</u> on the staff.
   The first is solved as an example.

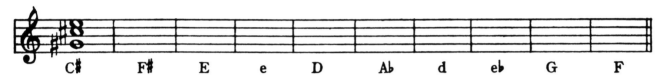

C#   F#   E   e   D   Ab   d   eb   G   F

3. Complete the following chords as indicated by the "figured bass". The first is solved as an example.

4. Complete the following chords as indicated by the "figured bass". The first is solved as an example.

5. Complete the following chords as indicated by the "figured bass". The first two are solved as an example.

Name_____

Drill Problems

Lesson 19.

1. Show, as in Example 69, the triads which occur in the key of
   "C minor" (harmonic form). Use a key signature. The 7th
   scale degree must be raised whenever it occurs. Label the
   chords with the Roman Numeral which correctly shows the
   triad type.

2. Spell the chords indicated in the chart. The first is solved
   as an example.

Key	Tonic	Subdominant	Dominant
F major	*f a c*	*bb d f*	*c e g*
B major			
C major			
f minor*			
D major			
E major			
d minor*			
g minor*			
Db major			

* Use harmonic form of the minor.

3. Indicate with Roman Numerals the triads that are <u>major</u> in major
   tonality. (a) _____ (b) _____ (c) _____.

4. Indicate the triads that are <u>minor</u> in major tonality.
   (a)_____ (b) _____ (c) _____.

5. Indicate the triad that is <u>diminished</u> in major tonality._____.

6. Indicate the triads that are <u>minor</u> in minor tonality (harmonic form). (a) _____ (b)_____.

(Cont'd.)   Name_____

Drill Problems, cont'd. (Lesson 19)

7. Indicate the triads that are <u>major</u> in minor tonality (harmonic form). (a) _____ (b) _____ .

8. Indicate the triads that are <u>diminished</u> in minor tonality
   (harmonic form). (a) _____ (b) _____ .

9. Indicate the triad that is <u>augmented</u> in minor tonality
   (harmonic form). (a) _____ .

10. Write, on the staff, the triads indicated. (Note that the
    key is given for each triad.) The first is solved as an
    example. (Large letters refer to major keys, small to minor
    keys.)

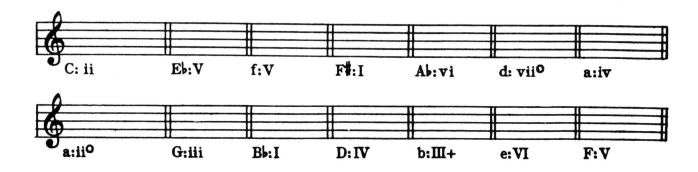

11. Label the following triads. The first is solved as an example.
    (Note that the key is given for each triad.)

Name _____